Nazarite Documents: comprising the obligations, practical propositions, lamentations, recommendations, &c. of the Nazarite Union of the Genesee Conference of the M.E. Church.

Published By
Nazarite Union of the Genesee
Conference of the M.E. Church.

First Fruits Press
Wilmore, Kentucky
c2017

Nazarite documents: comprising the obligations, practical propositions, lamentations, recommendations, &c. of the Nazarite Union of the Genesee Conference of the M.E. Church.

First Fruits Press, ©2017
Previously published by William Haswell, Printer, 1856.

ISBN: 9781621716433 (print), 9781621716440 (digital), 9781621716457 (kindle)

Digital version at http://place.asburyseminary.edu/freemethodistbooks/25/

Nazarite documents: comprising the obligations, practical propositions, lamentations, recommendations, &c. of the Nazarite Union of the Genesee Conference of the M.E. Church.-- Wilmore, Kentucky : First Fruits Press, ©2017.
    40 pages; 21 cm.
    Reprint. Previously published: Brockport, N.Y. : William Haswell, Printer, 1856.
    ISBN - 13: 9781621716433 (pbk.)
    1. Free Methodist Church of North America--History. 2. Methodist Episcopal Church. Genessee Conference--History. 3. Methodist Church--New York (State) 4. Methodist Church--Pennsylvania. I. Title.
BX8413.N39 2017   287.97

Cover design by Jon Ramsay

asburyseminary.edu
800.2ASBURY
204 North Lexington Avenue
Wilmore, Kentucky 40390

First Fruits
THE ACADEMIC OPEN PRESS OF ASBURY SEMINARY

First Fruits Press

The Academic Open Press of Asbury Theological Seminary

204 N. Lexington Ave., Wilmore, KY 40390

859-858-2236

first.fruits@asburyseminary.edu

asbury.to/firstfruits

NAZARITE DOCUMENTS:

COMPRISING

THE OBLIGATIONS, PRACTICAL PROPOSITIONS, LAMENTATIONS, RECOMMENDATIONS, &c.

OF THE

NAZARITE UNION,

OF THE

GENESEE CONFERENCE OF THE M. E. CHURCH.

BROCKPORT, N. Y.:

WM. HASWELL, PRINTER, HOLMES BLOCK, MAIN-ST.

1856.

PREFACE.

EXTRACTS FROM THE MINUTES OF A PRIMARY CONSULTATION OF SEVERAL PREACHERS IN FAVOR OF OLD LINE METHODISM.

Br. R. stated that, in his opinion, it had become necessary to have a closer union among ourselves in respect to the observance of the rules and customs of the Church. Especially as in certain quarters there seemed a set purpose to ignore the discipline and to bring in innovations upon the time-honored customs of the Fathers. The evil results of this were everywhere manifest. Isolated and individual effort in resistance had been tried, but with little success . The invading flood of innovation was too strong to be resisted by isolated individual effort. Either a vigorous and united effort at resistance must be made, or it were as well to give up at once and let the current of events keep on its " progress."

Br. W. stated that he had for years been aware of the " progressive " tendency of things, and had endeavored, as in conscience bound, and as bound also by his ordination vows, to " mind everything in the Discipline, both great and small;" and that in doing so he had several times found himself in a " fix " among a portion of the people, besides being several times also transfixed by his brethren in the ministry as a troubler in Israel. His own personal experience would corroborate the truth of the statement made by Br. R., that little if anything remedial could be hoped for from separate effort. He was aware of difficulties and obstacles far deeper and higher than were palpable to the view of younger men, and his opinion of late years, had become entirely doubtful as to the possibility of maintaining even what little of distinctive Methodistic usages were left us. Still he would not discourage younger brethren. It would do them no harm to learn for themselves, as he had for himself, by experience, the difficulty, and the danger also, of any *real and conscientious* efforts to conform to the discipline and usages of the Church. He would consent to be considered as a false prophet if they did not urge themselves into an experimental conviction that the days of proscription and persecution were not exclusively allotted to the earlier dispensations of Christianity. Nevertheless, though certain of the failure to accomplish the good proposed, and equally certain of the proscription incurred by the laudable attempt, he was willing to stand, as ever, alone, or with others who dare, in the old paths. It was early enough to say " A lion is in the way," when we could prove the fact by showing the scars of his teeth and claws.

Br. H. stated that he had ever been of the mind of the last speaker, and probably always should be. He had known him long and well, and where he had failed in the fight for God and Methodism it was the merest presumption in others to attempt to stand and stem the tide. It is dangerous in these days to be even suspected of strong and decided Methodistic attachments. Whoever experiences such attachment becomes a kind of "stump candidate " for Tunianguant, or some like stumpy circuit. The hue and cry of " old fogy " is " progressed " after him. The whole kennel open their bay upon him, and he is hunted like the last uncouth Mastodon, out of the world of modern and civilized Methodism. There may be some hope in the minds of some, from union and a combination of strength: but I can hardly believe its success. It will only enlarge the hunt and make it the more zealous.

Br. R.—But we shall stand at bay.

Br. H.—So much the worse. A steadier mark for the sporting gentry. But leaving this allusion: I am with the Discipline, and with the usages, and with the simplicity and spiritual power of old line Methodism, and with those brethren here, and the world over, who go in for this earnest christianity—this baptism of the washing of regeneration, which wets in to the *soul* and washes it out clean. This I am in favor of: and opposed with all my soul to this sham religion—this nominal religion, giving only the name into the Church—which exhibits its clerical professors in Odd Fellow regalia, " shawled to the nose and bearded to the eyes," reading foolscap sermons one day, and praying open secret lodges the next;—pipe-laying and managing in the Conference to oust out some, and hoist in others—and its lay professors rigged out in brass and feathers, and imitation posies, together with all its artifices to entice the world to love and support the Church: such as its sham donations, post-offices, lotteries, grab-bags, and oyster suppers for God. All these I am opposed to, and would do them away if I could. Against all these abominations I have warred a good warfare, I have fought a good fight, and have kept the faith I took upon me at my ordination, and I shall keep it to the end, which is not far off. I mean to go up to the General Conference and Assembly in the New Jerusalem above with clean hands in this matter. I am a disabled soldier; I can only hobble along in the ranks, leaning upon the sword of the Spirit as the staff of my feeble decline. I shall soon fail,— till then I am with you for God and Methodism, to hold a stake, or clinch a cord, as I may be able,—to help to strengthen the one and lengthen the other. And when I fall some of you will be by me. You will pray for me by my bedside, while I am wrestling with strong Death. One of you will preach my funeral sermon, and will tell the people that Br. H. has gone to heaven,—a sinner saved alone by grace.

After the singing of two verses of the hymn—

"And let this feeble body fail,"

Br. M. stated that the closing remarks of the preceding speaker had carried his thoughts almost beyond the present concerns. And it was well. The thoughts came back from the confines of that higher life, with a sweeter and sterner purpose to act well our part in this. And it will be well if all our thoughts and deeds here shall be in spiritual character and sympathy accordant with the spirit of that high and heavenly life to which we hope to come. But there are passage duties along the path of our pilgrimage. The perpetual obligation of vigilance and endurance is upon us. This not for ourselves alone, but for others also, lest we and they, seduced from the narrow way, fail of coming in at the end. There always has been a demand for such vigilance and endurance, and there always will be. This is the spiritual fitness of things. Nothing is impossible that is in harmony with God. Impossibility is a word that has no right in the Christian's vocabulary. Then let the idea of impossibility, in this matter, be discarded at once. But let us look the difficulties in the face. They are made to be overcome. We cannot croak them away. Some have tried that and have failed. We must *do* them away; and the more calmly and pleasantly the better. In the return to old line Methodism there are two prominent difficulties among our people. One is the introduction into the Church —in late years—of many who never knew anything about the earlier customs and spirit of Methodism; to whom its restitution would seem a novelty—a new kind of religion. This class may possibly include some preachers. This is a difficulty. Another is, the discouraged state of the older of the membership among us, growing out of our variant administration. One administrator practices according to the Book of Discipline, and another according to the patent inventions of the day; and the people, like an invalid under the treatment of two discordant doctors, in despair refuse the prescriptions of either, and ask only to be let alone to die in peace. This state of things is the main difficulty with our people. Patent doctors and their nostrums undo the health of the daughter of our people faster than disciplinary treatment can restore it. Hence this fatal discouragement. Croaking will not allay this. Audacious hope is useful here.

But the chief difficulties in the way of return to old line Methodism will be found from our brethren in the ministry. First from a lack of courage to observe and enforce the Discipline. This is *the* great obstacle. This obstacle looms up here in this consultation. It fills the whole horizon around, and is piled in clouds of discouragement to the zenith above. Doubtless many of the brethren would be glad to have both church and ministry live up to the Discipline. and observe the customs of the Church—but there is a lion in the way—or, in other words, the world, or that portion of it incorporated in the Church, is in the way. The Discipline always was an eye-sore to worldliness, either in the Church or out. And the strong temptation is to be at peace with the world by ignoring the Discipline.

Furthermore, there are progressive men among us who have found out an easier way to get along in than the old, uncompromising disciplining one. They look upon the world as having progressed wonderfully since their entrance into it; and Methodism must be progressed accordingly. That instead of conforming the world to God, it must conform itself to the world in order to lead the world more readily to God. All distinct spirituality must be purged away from the church, as distasteful to the world, and the church thus purged of the spiritual element so disgusting to the world, is to do wonders toward its conversion. This dogma is the *Alma-Mater* of all our worldly conformities in the face of the discipline. This is the mother of all our abominations, from the written sermons in the pulpit up to the screeching fiddle in the orchestra, away to the midnight conclave in the lodge, and down to the "sham post-offices, lotteries, grab-bags, and oyster suppers for God" in the basement or parsonage. All these things must be gone into to enlist the interests of the world in favor of an enlightened liberal and progressive Christianity, and to aid in spreading scriptural holiness over these lands by sweetening it with worldly alloy so entirely that the devil himself would swallow it without a qualm. This worldly conformity is of course contrary to the Discipline of the Church; and we may expect the most strenuous opposition in any disciplinary course, from these members and preachers who have unfortunately fallen into this way of doing things. Not that they will boldly in word ignore the Discipline, but their conduct in the case will be by implication impugned by a contrary example. We shall be charged with creating a division because we get some to observe the discipline and customs of the church, while others will not do it, nor suffer others to do it without raising a fuss about it. But we ought to bear in mind that the Discipline is the Rule of our conduct as preachers. The obligation is upon us to adhere to it; and if others see fit to rage and revile, and proscribe because we purpose to adhere to it, we are not responsible for that. That is not our business. But nothing can be done alone. There must be a union of purpose and conduct in the case. We must renew our ordination vows with special emphasis, to keep them whether the world is willing or not. For one I am ready to do so, let what will come. I am ready to stand anywhere I am put in this behalf.

Br. K. stated that not only the formal Rules and customs of the church were much neglected among us; such as attendance on the more spiritual means of grace, and the prohibition of metalic and feathery, and other artificial ornamentals, or regimentals as they might be called; but there was serious danger that the distinctive doctrines of Methodism, by these leading strings of the old Enemy be led away also. The doctrine of Christian perfection had already come to be so mystified, as to be the subject of newspaper quarrels, notwithstanding what Wesley, Fletcher, Clarke, and other of the fathers had so clearly and explicitly written. The departure from the Rules of the Church he conceived to be the open door out of which its doctrines would depart, unless the door was closed. He believed the original Wesleyan Church was declared to be a company "having the form and seeking the power of Godliness."— They were united together in this form and in this purpose. He conceived the M. E. Church in all its membership and ministry included in the original bond to this. Whatever others might do, he wished it clearly understood that he "belongs to this band, Hallelujah!"

Br. E. stated that he was a quiet man, and had never had any trouble in enforcing the discipline; for the reason he supposed, that he had never enforced it. He tried to preach the gospel and persuade saints and sinners to get religion, and had been somewhat successful, but not as much so as he ought to have been. He had probably showed more respect to the Discipline than some, for he had not inveighed against it; and not so much as some for he had never enforced it. In this respect he believed he stood with a respectable number if not a majority of his brethren. For himself he was not a *forcible* man; especially in disciplinary administration. He wished to be with his brethren in the matter, and would neither go ahead nor lag behind. He apprehended no great difficulty in the case, provided all would concur to keep the Rules, as they had promised to do. But the difficulty was, some tried to be a little close, and others let everything run loose, and the people knew not what to do. After several years of neglect it was a sort of a hardship to them to be straightened up, ever so little, to the rules of the Church;

and possibly the next year or two to fall back into the same neglect. It discouraged those who were seeking for the old paths. He tho't as long as we had Rules it was best to be governed by them—a little, at least. The great want in the case was uniformity; and he was ready to uniform, and hoped all the others would also; and make a general and united business of it. He had noticed that the work of the Lord had prospered most where the Rules were most closely kept. He was in favor of a general conspiracy to resuscitate old line Methodism. He thought nobody could have any objection to that.

The above extracts are deemed a sufficient preface to the "Nazarite Roll" as it was called at the last Conference, which follows. It was read before the Conference, in accordance with a resolution of that body calling for the reading of all papers relating to the (so called) Nazarites. Several private and confidential letters to different preachers, relating to the matter were also procured and read in connection with the "Roll." They are omitted out of respect to the feelings of those to whom they were addressed; and also for the further reason that some of them involve personalities. The Nazarite matter at the last Conference created quite a sensation—probably more than was necessary—and was variously represented and misrepresented. The "Roll" will speak for itself; and is the only authorized exponent of the principles of the old line Methodists of the Genesee Conference, who have been proclaimed abroad as Nazarites, by the publishers of the Minutes of the Conference, and by the Buffalo Advocate. Those papers are responsible for the publication of the name. It is supposed to be intended to describe those who are "sticklers for trifles"—such as the more stringent and severe rules of the Church. One of the preachers of the Conference, as the writer of the "Roll," and of the correspondence pertertaining to it, has been charged with "crimes sufficient to exclude a person from the Kingdom of Grace and Glory" stated in *thirty-nine* specifications—"forty stripes save one"—founded on statements in the Roll and its relative correspondence, and also three "falsehoods." So the work of proscription is commenced and will doubtless continue till it ends—itself. A certain pamphlet published in New York, has represented the Nazarites as a secret society devoted to the propagation of doctrinal tenets. It is enough to say that its author has been imposed upon by his zealous correspondent; both as to the fact and purpose of the Nazarites. It is only as yet a mere *proposal* to return to the "old paths."

NAZARITE UNION.

HISTORIC CIRCULAR.

BRETHREN:—The notion of an united and orderly effort to re-turn more fully, as ministers, to the observance and enforcement of the Discipline of the Church, and to the religious customs of early Methodism has been in the minds of several for two years past. Some were decided for immediate action;—but some hesitated dreading the imputation of partizanship in the Conference. They dreaded also the inevitable hostility to the measure from a certain quarter, as it was foreseen to be necessary to disturb the feelings and plans of a very enterprising, unscrupulous and vindictive fraternity in our midst, which held the ear of the Episcopacy, and by secret and adroit man-agement wielded, for the time being, the chief patronage of the Con-ference. At length, however, the number concurring being about twelve, it was resolved to form the Union, and solicit the co-opera-tion of all those preachers in the Conference whose antecedents and sympathies were judged to be in favor of a return to "the old paths —the paths our fathers trod."

Although the *obligation* proposed enjoins no secrecy, it is never-theless advisable that, till the matter shall be thoroughly spread be-fore those indicated, a discreet silence be observed; both to avoid noise and confusion, which in religious matters above all others, ought to be avoided, and also to prevent a premature outcry from frightening some of our less resolute brethren from a co-operation before they fully understand the matter. Thus far the Union has been accomplished through the agency of District consultations: it being of course impossible to get many of the preachers together.

Thus far, by tacit refusal, no Odd Fellow has been solicited; and by common consent, thus far, none will be admitted except on convincing proof satisfactory to all that he holds his obligations to the Church superior to his obligations to the Lodge, and will not, by obligation or sympathy, act with them in *their* management of Conference or Church affairs. No Presiding Elder is solicited or admitted, because of his official position, which might be thought to be embarrassed thereby. A simple and scriptural device, the hint of which was taken from the tenth chapter of Nehemiah, was formed, both as a token of union, and as a defence provided any one chose to keep it secret, against Odd Fellow vengeance; in anticipation of such being threatened and attempted to be executed. At first it was proposed to have *three divisions;* and some circulars were issued with this view —but on more general consultation this was abandoned as unnecessary and liable to excite prejudice. All the traveling preachers subscribing the *obligation,* with the limitation above recited, are acknowledged members, and of equal rights, privileges and powers in the Union. The general officers annually to be appointed by the whole body, are a President, a Recorder, a Chief Scribe, and one Scribe and one Counsellor in each District. These constitute the Executive Committee of the Union, to circulate the obligation and documents: to encourage the brethren in the several Districts in the good work, and to give them such advice and counsel in all things pertaining to the objects of the Union, as the exigencies of circumstances may demand, in respect to the manner of its execution. It is not designed to spread any organization among the people. The aim is to return gradually and surely to the old paths, without strife or divisions, other than that which will necessarily arise from the spontaneous conflict of sentiment between persons of adverse views in respect to the general propriety of the general object proposed.

This is all the Order, Organization, Society or Band, contemplated by the "Nazarites" of the Genesee Conference. We hold such a Society to be no more improper than a " Preachers' Aid Society"— or a " Preachers' Anti-Slavery Society." This Nazarite Union might appropriately be styled a " Preachers' Come-back-to-the-Discipline Society," for it is that and nothing else.

NAZARITE OBLIGATION.

1.—I will observe and enforce the Rules of the Methodist Episcopal Church to the best of my ability, and under all practicable circumstances.
2.—I will steadfastly resist all departures from them, or from the religious customs derived therefrom.
3.—I will steadfastly oppose the introduction or continuance among us of any religious practice or custom or of any institution foreign to, or at variance with the Discipline of the Church.
4.—And I will encourage and sustain, in the disciplinary execution of the above purpose, in preference to all others, those covenanting together in this obligation.

PRACTICAL PROPOSITIONS.

1.—To restore the observance of the Rules requiring attendance on Class.
2.—To restore the observance of the Rules requiring family prayer.
3.—To restore the observance of the Rules requiring quarterly fasts.
4.—To restore the observance of the Rules requiring singing by the congregation.
5.—To restore the custom, in part, of free seats in our houses of worship.
6.—To restore the custom of attendance from abroad upon our Love Feasts.
7.—To restore the custom of Camp Meetings more fully among us.
8.—To restore, generally, simplicity and spirituality in our worship.

The above is a true copy of the Obligation and Practical Propositions of the Nazarite Union of the Genesee Conference, as revised and approved in the last general consultation.

J. M^C CREARY, Jr.,
Chief Scribe.

THE GENERAL ARGUMENT.

Dear Brethren:—Come and let us reason together. Let us speak of the state of Methodism among us. Let us do so calmly, truthfully, earnestly. Let us not be afraid to think, to see, to speak; and to act also, as the great occasion may demand. There is a patriotism above that which has respect to our native land—our civil inheritance; a patriotism whose sleepless hopes and fears walk their perpetual rounds about Mount Zion, the city of our inheritance spiritual, and watch intently the safety of her bulwarks, as the defence of her flaming altars. If these fall, those are extinguished.

Methodism has been the great religious power of the century past, and it remains so still when compared with other religious denominations. The religious sentiment of Methodism is the religious sentiment of the million masses. They believe her doctrines. They sympathise with all her feelings and movements. They hail her as the great religious instrumentality of the age. They love her, for she speaks to them in their mother tongue of the wonderful works of God. Other denominations cause them to listen; she causes them to hear. They, in learned phrase, whisper to the ear; she, in thunder tones of simple yet wondrous power, rolls her glorious message right through the living heart of the mighty people. This power is her heritage from Him "whose is the kingdom and the power." "Holiness unto the Lord," written in light upon her spotless garments, and engraved upon her frontlets, is the significant motto of her mission to spread scriptural holiness through these lands. These were the benediction words of her inauguration and the commandment for her administration. Commissioned thus by Almighty God himself, and commanded to overcome every obstacle, she was expected to be invincible and victorious: and the hopes of heaven and of earth, gathered upon her, that not till the final accomplishment of this mission, and in full view of the chariot of her translation would she drop the mystic mantle of her prophetic power, and turn aside from, or grow weary in the work which was given her to do. But, alas, her pathway of destiny lay along the enchanted ground of "modern progress," and there, fallen asleep from her mighty work, she has lost the roll from her bosom. Her Discipline is gone. Shall she return and find it? Or shall she endeavor to make progress without it? Shall it be recovered and carried with her; or, leaving it behind as burdensome, or as antiquated and useless, or as irrecoverably lost, shall she endeavor to go up and prosper without it? This is the question.

It is a melancholy pleasure to look back from the uncertain present upon the stern and glorious past of our beloved Methodism, and note her triumphant progress throughout the first century of her mission. "Beauty and Bands"—purity of heart, and strict discipline of life—were the two staves of her strength through all her way of spiritual conquest. They never dropped from her hands for a moment. They were held fast with all the tenacity of life, with all the rigidity of death. And well might they be; for they were the implements not of her power only, but of her safety also. From her first advent upon American soil already pre-occupied with adverse and bigoted doctrines and sentiments, it required strong and uncompromising men to lead the van of her array. And she found such men. No flinching from controversy—no craven spirit of compromise — no dread of perils and starvation in the wilderness—no fears of popular commotions—no yielding to finical and artificial godliness—no vibrating between God and Mammon; right onward they drove the chariot of this salvation through all the land. "There were giants in those days;" for the times required gigantic men—spiritual Titans—to unpile the mountain obstacles rising in the way of truth and righteousness. And the best of all was, God was with them; for they were with God. In all their trials and labors, the unseen Power—the King immortal, invisible, eternal, was their support. Right behind them, ever sounding after them, that serene and awful voice "Lo, I am with you," came with its mighty impulse, and urged them on to the victorious strife. In the midst of all this success it is on record that those early fathers of Methodism were strict disciplinarians. They observed and enforced the Discipline for conscience sake. Their vows to do so were not lightly taken, as a kind of formal rubric necessary to ordination, to be violated according to convenience or inclination; but with a *bona fide* intention to observe and keep them. They were true men; not in word only, but in deed also. And the spiritual quality of the membership revealed the faithfulness of the ministry in this respect. The dead, as soon as they were decently cold, were buried out of sight, and not left in the midst of the living, to breed pestilence and death: and thus the health of the daughter of our people was preserved. No undisciplinary innovations were allowed —no exempt cases—they were nipped in the bud, before a rank and luxuriant growth had rendered them unmanageable. Everywhere, and under all circumstances, justification by faith, sanctification by the Spirit, and conformity of life to the Discipline, were exhorted as the privilege, and demanded as the duty of every member of the church. Such were the men—the early grandees of the realm of Methodism—who maintained its glory by maintaining its integrity; who gained its victories by disciplining its legions. But they are gone; and with them the first century of Methodism;—an hundred years of unparalleled progress and prosperity; which during the century to come must necessarily be infinitely augmented or diminished as we shall either follow or repudiate their example.

Notwithstanding the croakings of veteran backsliders, who, chiefly because they are backslidden, imagine the church to have become, since their early days, hopelessly apostate; and notwithstanding, on the other hand, the hopeful eulogies and anticipations of some less observing and more enthusiastic, it is the sober and solemn conviction of many among us, especially of those whose antecedents reach along the line of earlier Methodism into the past, that there are some just reasons for alarm as respects the present, and of forbodings for the future. Those reasons are palpable, and certainly sufficient in interest to attract attention, and demand appropriate action. In the southern and western conferences, for obvious reasons, growing out of social circumstances, and the maintainance practically as well as nominally of its itineracy, Methodism yet retains nearly or quite its original status and complexion. But it is undeniable that in this conference it has been for several years past assuming a kind of hybrid form—and is still in a sort of transition state, vibrating between original principles and those transcendental and anomalous innovations, which are a striking characteristic of the age through which we are passing. "Vanity Fair" is outspread all around us; and many of us, preachers and people, are exchanging our pilgrim garb, and our titles to the inheritance of the saints in light, in barter for the empty baubles offered to our purchase.

All that is left of the Discipline among us, are here and there a few feeble and uncertain attempts to observe some of its most general prescriptions; and those the least calculated to annoy worldly-minded professors. The rules respecting class meetings are hardly ever enforced, except against such as have become too dead to feel indignant at their application. The rules respecting family prayer, quarterly fasts, singing in the congregation, pewed churches, and the manner of our love feasts, have gradually, by neglect of enforcement fallen into disuse. Some of the ministry speak openly of the legislative abrogation of the whole, and seem determined to prepare the way therefor, by ignoring them altogether in their administration. The Discipline is virtually dead and buried, and its sepulchre is among us at this day, while the few feeble and desultory efforts to restore it is the stone upon its mouth. Such is the general hopelessness of its restitution among those in the ministry and membership, who would be glad to see it restored, that they are tempted to yield up in despair to its total abandonment, as a calamity compelled by the evil force of irresistible circumstances. Even the strong men among us—the fathers—as if in dread of the ready charge of being sticklers for trifles; or the charge of superstitious fondness for obsolete antiquities, have given way to the tide of ridicule against it and them, and leave the Discipline to its fate by merely exhorting its observance, and conniving at its neglect by those in the ministry under their supervision. Meanwhile we have turned every way to find a substitute. Thus far we have signally failed. We have improved our financial plans,—we have increased in number and convenience our church edifices,—we have labored successfully to elevate the standard of ministerial education;—in fine, we have done everything we could do, besides attempting many things we could not do, to regain our former power. Thus far in vain. If there be a substitute for the Discipline it remains yet to be found.

Let us more particularly cast our attention upon the condition of the Church as superinduced by this fatal neglect of Discipline. During the seven years past the increase of membership in this Conference has been less than one per cent per annum. It is also obvious to a strict observer of the condition of things, that there has been a gradual decay in the spirit of vital and active godliness.— This is strikingly apparent in our larger stations, more exposed to worldly associations, and more contemptuous of disciplinary obligations. While our secular concerns as a Church have been receiving the temporary impulses of extraordinary efforts in behalf of their prosperity, the great fundamental principle of spirituality has languished more and more. In some of the charges above referred to, any manifestations of spiritual influence have become so strange and uncommon as to be mistaken for fanaticism;—even those spiritual exercises so common among us in our earlier history as a denomination. Not even a decent form of godliness remains, much less its power. The old, reliable, working, praying, singing, shouting fathers and mothers are gone;—some to sing and shout in heaven:—some have removed to other lands,—some have laid down in the dust, discouraged, to croak and die. A few yet remain, thank God, in our midst, the real strength of our Zion. But the proportional number of such has gradually decreased from year to year, and our ranks have been filled up by such as, for the most part, have been merely *imagined* into the Church; not, as formerly, converted weepingly, prayingly, shoutingly, triumphantly, decidedly:— but, at the best, faintly converted, sickly and silent from the birth, and ever retaining that same original, hereditary silence and feebleness.

Our periodicals teem with grandiloquent notices of revivals of this sort, generally with a superadded notice ingeniously interwoven of preachers, elders, wandering evangelists, and other fine and powerful things instrumental in the great and glorious work. The names of the converts are recorded on the class books. For a few weeks, or possibly a few months, they attend the class and prayer meetings, and then gradually fade away and die from whatever little of spiritual life they may have once possessed. They remain, still, nominal members of the Church. They count as such in our annual Conference reports. Adorned in artificial, if not in costly array, they "sit in beauty side by side," in our galleries, and in the rear of our congregations. But their voice is never heard in our love feasts, our class meetings, or our prayer meetings. The only religious service in which they ever deign to engage is that of singing the praises of God for us, whenever their fancy or pride prompts them to do so; provided, furthermore, they are allowed the exclusive monopoly of this service. Any effort to save or restore their spiritual life, by bringing to even a common observance of our healthful and life-preserving disciplinary rules is usually unavailing, from the desultory efforts and adverse views of the several administrators of the same. Any attempt at excision is shunned by us as endangering our reputation as "fine" ministers among the people, and as "safe" men in the cabinet;—the last appellation being generally, the honorable title, well earned among us, of such as have the common prudence, never seriously to assault the world, the flesh, or the devil. Instances have been known among us, where rich fathers, veteran members of the Church, have threatened to withdraw in case their backslidden children were molested by the application of the Discipline. And the shameful record is required by the truth that such threats are generally, if not always successful to prevent its application. The Japanese teach their children to trample upon the Cross; we allow ours to trample upon the Discipline. Thus is slowly and surely accumulating upon us a membership educated for rebellion and insubordination, which will render a return to the Discipline more and more difficult, if not positively impossible as time advances.

In some of our chief charges, by some of our chief ministers, the Discipline is not read in the congregation or the society, according to its express prescription in the case. The quarterly fasts are never mentioned, and of course never observed. Societies counted by hundreds of members, furnish less than a score in the class meetings; and fewer still in the prayer meetings. Many members live without family prayer, or even the religious decency of asking a blessing at table. Officers in the Church, on grounds of secular economy, or from favoritism to exotic fraternities, are appointed of men never found in the exercise of religious worship other than a mere silent attendance on preaching. The singing, together with the selection of the final hymn,—if hymn it can be called—is politely delivered over to the control and "performance" of half a dozen young backsliders, to the exclusion of the right and prescribed duty of the membership to join in this service. A few members, of some wealth it may be, or of some superannuated religious reputation, or of some secular order fraternal with the pastor, and aided more or less by his encouragement or connivance, succeed in ruling the membership into their own views of worldly policy, and as far as possible into their own spirit. A cold and dry formality without even the redeeming quality of aristocratic dignity, so pervades the entire worship that those yet retaining any sense of the life and power of religion, feel that they can enjoy it any where else better than in the house of God.

One after another of the old members crawls off disheartened, to die; thus diminishing unit by unit the little sum of spirituality left. Add to all this the manifold dissentions between the various leading worldly minded members, originating in their pride of opinion, and adverse fancies in respect to their several schemes to glorify the Church and themselves, and we have before us, as far as it goes, a true description of many of our chief societies—societies which, from being considered the pre-eminences of our Zion, exert, by their fatal example, a controlling influence throughout the Conference at large. It is a fearful truth and cannot be disguised, that many of our principal sanctuaries within our bounds, are at this hour like the Pyramids of Egypt, each at once a temple and a tomb, filled with spiritual mummies, embalmed in the odor of a lifeless sanctity, awaiting in silence the vain hope of a resurrection they shall never see; while the preacher's voice, compelled by the power of association, and the craven fear of offense, is smoothed and softened, and lessened down to a reptile's whimper in these habitations of the dead.

And why is it thus? Is the arm of the Lord shortened that he cannot save? Do not the essential principles of Methodism remain the same? Have we not still the Ark of the Covenant with our tribe in the Commonwealth of Israel, and is there not the living fire in its glorious Urim still? Is not the Gospel still, as ever, the power of God unto salvation? And has not our number in the ministry largely increased in proportion to our membership? thus giving us the ability to bestow the more labor upon our work. Why, then, do we labor for nought? Nay, why for less than nought?—Brethren! we know the reason. "The stone wall thereof is broken down," and all our labor in the vineyard of the Lord is left defenceless to the ravages of the destroyer. And many among us, who from position should be master workmen in rebuilding it, not only shun the laborious and unpopular task themselves, but ridicule and discourage it in others,—discourage it as a vain and impossible attempt to resist the rush of modern progress,—ridicule it as an insane and superstitious adherence to principles and customs, essentially obsolete forever, because adapted only to the past. They have other masonic duties than building the walls of Jerusalem; other tents to pitch than the goodly tents of Jacob. After a century of triumphant test, it has at length been discovered by some of our leading ministers that the Discipline of our Church is a failure; that it is an antique incompatibility—incompetent to meet the exigencies of these more redundant times. And it is lamentable to know, and shameful to record that the most efficient opponents to the Discipline in our midst are those very men who have been solemnly constituted its guardians,—who in the presence of God and the Conference

have publicly and voluntarily taken upon them special vows of adherence to it. These are the men whom the finical and worldly
minded in the Church and its outside hangers-on ever find to be
zealous and powerful coadjutors in every effort to void, or resist, or
over-ride the long tried customs of the Church, and the spirit and
letter of its recognized ecclesiastical law;—and he who, beholding
the living membership piled with heaps of the dead—imbedded
and inslimed in the mass of pestilential putridity—has the courage
and the commanding sense of disciplinary duty to seek and extri-
cate and separate them that they may live;—is sure, while engaged
in this work, to be cloven down from behind by the unseen hands of
such in the ministry. So that it has passed into a proverb among
us, that " he who attempts the enforcement of the Discipline within
the bounds of the Genesee Conference, is starved in his circuit, and
damned in the Conference."

Indeed, the chief difficulty in the way of our return to the old
paths is found at this point. The ministry have educated the people to neglect the Discipline by introducing or suffering practices
contrary to it, and when the people of any charge thus educated
experience a change of administration in which the Discipline is
somewhat recognized, preachers have been known to excite the people to rebellion against it, both as an apology for their past neglect
of its administration, and as a plea for neglecting it in future, on the
pretence that the *people* will not endure it in these enlightened
days of modern progress. By searching closely, the " hand of
Joab," is found in almost all commotions among the people, growing out of disciplinary administration among us.

In this connexion, brethren, we deem it our duty to ourselves and
to the cause of God, to be fully aware that by a strange coincidence,
hardly accidental, and yet possibly so, rather than from any intrinsic
pravity in the institution itself, most of those among us thus occupying position adverse to the Discipline, have the accompanying
misfortune to be connected together in a secret secular association,
whose oaths are unknown to the Discipline, and whose various obligations are generally held to be supreme as against any merely
ecclesiastical obligation whatever. The leading spirits in this fraternity have for several years been observed as the leaders in the
path of retrogression from the discipline and usages of the Church,
and as having arrayed almost its entire strength in the same
adverse attitude. We apprehend it may not be so in other
Conferences; and there are a few honorable exceptions in this,
of men who hold their vows made unto God and the Church,
superior in obligation to vows plighted in darkness to a fellowship which, to say the best, is not purely " the fellowship of
saints." When all these things are known to be so, who, especially among our younger preachers, will dare SINGLY to attempt his duty in the case? Who that has attempted the fulfill-

ment of his ordination vows, during the past five years, has escaped proscription, and the ruin of his ministerial reputation? What hope from variant and scattered efforts in the face of these formidable obstacles? None whatever. As soon might the Temperance reform have been accomplished by isolated effort. As soon might a few straggling Jews have rebuilt the walls of Jerusalem in the face of Sanballat the Horonite. There must be a *union* of steadfast purpose and persistent effort among the preachers to return to the observance of the rules and customs of the Church, or we shall never return. Let no man flatter himself to the contrary. Such a union we propose, and nothing else.

N. B. Those brethren to whom this paper may come, will closely observe the accompanying documents, and from time to time give such counsel as they may deem proper, which may be rendered either to the Recorder or the Chief Scribe of the Union. The documents alluded to above will be issued from the Recorder.

LAMENTATIONS AND RECOMMENDATIONS.

PRACTICAL PROPOSITION No. 1.

" To restore the observance of the Rules requiring attendance on Class Meetings."

LAMENTATION :—Alas for the general neglect of Class Meetings! It has been gradually increasing upon us for the last seven years.— In some of our charges societies counted by hundreds of members furnish only a score or less who attend Class with any degree of punctuality. In many charges attendance is considered a mere matter of convenience or inclination. The ancient sense of privilege or duty in the case has subsided from the minds of our people.— Leaders have become discouraged and have ceased to mark their books. Doubtless four-fifths of the Class Books in the Conference are not regularly marked from year to year. Preachers have scolded over this neglect of Class Meetings, Bishops have lamented over it in their addresses to the Conferences. District Associations and Quarterly Conferences have complained and resolved. Still the evil grows steadily upon us. A fearful accumulation of lifeless member-ship has gathered upon the surface of the Church from this fatal neglect. What is still more lamentable than all, those converted under the ministry of the Word among us, not being held as in for-mer years to this exercise, soon fade away and die from spiritual life.

What shall be done to remedy this evil? There are difficulties in the way. No other evil among us is so enormous as this. It is more general than any other. Neglect of Class Meetings has made backsliders numerous; and they in return render it extreme-ly difficult to enforce attendance on Class. They hate the Class Room. Many of them would sooner leave the Church than attend Class once a quarter. Some of them are rich; some are respectable; some are men of secular ability, available to the Church financially; some are officers in the Church,—stewards or trustees. Charges are small and weak; financial embarrassments render every available help necessary. We carry on a heavy stroke of business. Our ex-tensive co-partnership with the world has rendered rich men neces-sary to us. The valedictory as foreboded by Wesley has been spo-ken. "Farewell to Methodist Discipline, if not to Methodist doc-trine also." Our bread is in our mouth, as preachers. It will not do to offend the rich. They will starve us if we do. If we in-sist on their attendance they will be offended and we starved. But if we suffer them to neglect Class we must suffer all; we must be impartial in the matter. Thus the rich are a shield to the poor in transgressing the Rules with impunity. Besides this we dread dis-turbance in societies; we fear the imputation of being troublers in Israel; we dread the ready charge of rashness, obstinacy, radicalism, ultraism, &c., &c., which is sure to be elicited by any attempt seri-ously to remedy the evil. We love bread and the praise of men; while hundreds are annually perishing from the way of life through our neglect of enforcing the Discipline in the case. A strong cen-tral tower of our Zion has fallen in the dust, who will arise and build? *This is our lamentation.*

RECOMMENDATION:—Let all the Class Books be revised imme-diately after Conference. Let the Leaders be kindly and closely reasoned with, and encouraged and required to mark their books regularly. Let the Preacher, once a quarter immediately preceding the Quarterly Meeting, read before the Class, Society, or congrega-tion, the number of times each member has attended Class during the quarter; and at the same time inquire of the Leader, formally, the cause of any noticeable absence. Let the Class books be laid upon the table of the Quarterly Meeting Conference, that the Pre-siding Elder may examine them. This will show the Leaders and members that some notice is taken of their conduct in respect to this duty. This will have its influence; for duties with appropriate and palpable accountability, are not apt to be neglected. Let the Discipline in the case be read before the congregation once a quarter. Before the congregation; otherwise many members might not hear it as read before the Class, or Society. Let the reading precede the second hymn. It will occupy but little time. At the same time let the Preacher inform the membership that he is bound by his ordination vows to enforce the Discipline, however repugnant it may be to his personal feelings. At the first, such is the general and habitual neglect of this duty, and such our exceeding laxity of past administration in the case, let him *insist* on the attendance of each member at least one-third of the time. This without any intimation of license to refrain at all; but as a show and fact of moderation and to avoid all reasonable grounds of charge of undue strictness in administration. Let all cases of sickness, distance, and other providential hindrances be taken benignly into consideration, and then if there be not a coming up, in any one quarter, to the one-third attendance above specified, let the Discipline take its course—in every case—against rich and poor, great and small. "Be very mild but very firm."

In some charges the Sunday School is appointed at the regular hour most convenient for the Class Meetings. Here is a dilemma to be avoided if possible. One department of our work ought not to interfere with another. It will not do to rob the Sunday School in behalf of the Class Meeting, nor the Class Meeting in behalf of the Sunday School. Our younger members most in need of this means of grace, are usually connected with the Sunday School. Some, growing more or less backslidden, soon learn to prefer the Sunday School, as a refuge from the distasteful obligations and exercises of the Class room. Thus, while we acknowledge the Sunday School to be the nursery of the Church, it is to be feared that in the way above indicated, by being placed in competition, as to time, with the Class Meeting, it may have robbed the Church of many a goodly plant of larger growth. This is a delicate and doubtful point,—a point in which the right and utility must be determined by contingent circumstances. Our conclusion is that the class meeting is *first—first* in the Discipline—*first* in power for spiritual utility. The officers and children of our Sunday Schools, being members, ought not to be deprived from it. There is no Discipline to absolve them from attendance. And on the other hand, our faithful, Class-loving membership ought not to be deprived from working in the Sunday School, or attending the Bible Class, by the simultaneous Class Meeting. Then let the Sabbath School be in the morning, if otherwise it interferes with the Sabbath noon Class Meetings. It will gain more than it will lose from the increased attendance and interest in it of the adult membership. This especially if the officers, teachers, and children cannot conveniently attend other than the Sabbath noon Classes. Let all our Sunday School children be encouraged to attend Class Meeting, as members *ex officio* of the Church. We venture this liberal construction of the Discipline in their behalf. — *This is our recommendation.*

PRACTICAL PROPOSITION No. 2.

" To restore the observance of the Rules requiring Family Prayer."

LAMENTATION:—Alas for the neglect of family prayer among us. This neglect is the usual accompaniment of the neglect of other religious duties. Very many of our members are guilty of it. In some of our charges, even Stewards, to the great scandal of the church, live without family prayer, and thus cast the shadow of their evil example over the private membership. What a fatal example before children also! What avails Sunday School instruction against home example? How few of those children converted in our meetings, long survive the fatal atmosphere of a prayerless home! We have been at fault in this matter. We are not bold to reprove and exhort. We have failed to encourage leaders to examine their members on this duty. We have not pressed it with sufficient earnestness upon all heads of families converted among us. Alas! we have feared to do our duty to prayerless members. Some are rich; oppressed with worldly cares, and absorbed in worldly labors. We fear to offend them. They give us our daily bread; and we eat it, winking at their delinquencies in this duty. The Rule has become practically obsolete as against every offender. In addition to this, many of our members are without even the common religious decency of asking a blessing at table. A traveller stopping over night with them, would not even suspect them of making a profession of religion. We have many such among us. *This is our lamentation.*

RECOMMENDATION:—Exhort every head of a family, who may be converted among us, to the discharge of this duty. Encourage him to it. Insist upon it. Receive none into full connexion who fail in this. Acknowledge no backslider, in the church or out of it, as reclaimed, till he take to the discharge of this duty. No man, however rich or respectable is worth retaining who neglects. The more influential he is, the more fatal his example. In leading the classes inquire of every member. Let none escape. Report in the quarterly conference before the presiding elder all official members who are delinquent. Nominate no steward, on any plea whatsoever who is delinquent. Here is occasion for the strictest adherence to the charge "be diligent." What is Sunday religion without religion at home? This is not a small matter. Let us see to it. *This is our recommendation.*

PRACTICAL PROPOSITION No. 3.

" To restore the observance of the Rules requiring Quarterly Fasts."

LAMENTATION:—Alas for the neglect of fasting or abstinence among us! It was once our regular and prevalent custom. We were noted for it. We were benefitted by it as a people. It helped our religious meditations. It made a breach in the train of our worldly thoughts. It drew our hearts from the world. Its tendency was to prepare our minds for the solemn Quarterly Meeting exercises. This custom is now almost totally abandoned by us. The preachers themselves generally neglect it. Many of them consider it an antiquated and superstitious custom. It is not observed in their families, either when they are at home or absent. It is forgotten. It is rarely proclaimed from the pulpit. It has ceased to be observed among us, except by a few of the more aged ministers and members, who remember the former days. Possibly we have not wilfully neglected; but we have at least carelessly neglected this duty. *This is our lamentation.*

RECOMMENDATION:—Let us announce each Quarterly Fast in the congregation boldly—as though we were not ashamed of it, even before a polite and worldly assembly. Let us repeat the announcement in the classes, and call on all who will return to the custom to manifest it by a rising vote. Let us thus commit the people to its observance: a recommittal to the observance of the Discipline in the case. Above all, let us observe it ourselves as an example to them. Let all the members of our families observe it—children and all. In these days of deplorable laxity let us set a rigid example. Let not the Moslem and heathen rebuke us by their superior religious devotion in this duty. Let us by all possible means show our earnest interest in this matter. It is no trifling custom of the Church. There is more in it than appears at first view. The Bible enjoins it. The Discipline commands it. Let it be observed.— *This is our recommendation.*

PRACTICAL PROPOSITION No. 4.

" To restore the observance of the Rules requiring singing by the congregation."

LAMENTATION:—Alas, for the silence that has come over us!—
Our harps are hung upon the willows. The inhabitants of the
rock have ceased to sing; and at the same time they have ceased to
shout from the tops of the mountains. It was not so in our earlier
days. Beyond all other people, the powerful gift of sacred song
was once ours. A stream of living melody, outpoured from the
souls of the Wesleys, flowed over and into the myriad hearts of
those whom God gave them as seals to their ministry. Wherever
the early fathers of Methodism moved, the desert and solitary place
was glad for them, and the land broke forth into singing as they
passed. But we have wasted this holy heritage. We have sold
our ancient birthright of song for the fictitious and soulless canticles
of the modern orchestra. Not now as of old do the songs of Zion
ring through our habitations at morn and at even tide, and enliven
our daily toil. Not as of old are they heard in our social religious
gatherings. Our class meetings and prayer meetings feel the
empty void they have left. We have ceased almost at once to sing
and to live. We have been beguiled of this our treasure, by a barter of trash;—and the bill of this profitless trade has been sanc-
tioned more or less by the princes of our Israel.

The prescriptions of the Discipline in the case are positive and
unmistakable. The whole matter and manner of singing is undeniably left under the hand of the preacher. The prescribed obligation rests on him alone. He may not surrender it into the hand of
others without a palpable breach of trust. But we have in many
cases surrendered it to the exclusive control of the vain and frivolous
among us—to those for the most part whose voice is never heard in
our prayer meetings, our class meetings, our love feasts; whose only
religious service in which they ever deign to engage is that of per-
forming in solemn burlesque the praises of God for us, whenever
their fancy or pride prompts them to do so. This departure from
our Rules on singing has had a great tendency not only to impair
the spirituality of our worship, by banishing from it a vital element, but it has also ever been a prolific source of petty strife, small
pride, formality and various congenial and ever attendant confusions.
It is a common thing for a Choir to die and revive several times a
year. A petty jealousy among its members, then a pout, then a
roar, then a dissolution, then a reconciliation; to be followed by suc-
cessive pouts, roars, and dissolutions;— meanwhile the solemn worship of God in this vital department is left subject to all the disgusting
and scandalous influences of these orchestral vicissitudes. And the
worst feature of the case is, if the Choir see fit to become defunct at
any time, or to be absent, we are left blankly at their mercy, from

our having lost the general habit of singing. We have neglected to improve this gift, having surrendered all occasion and opportunity for its exercise. We have buried this talent—hid it in the butterfly's nest in the gallery of the temple. We have, as a people, neglected to furnish ourselves with "Our Hymn Book," having voided our privilege to use it for its appropriate purpose. From the stately temple in our chief cities to the veriest outside school house appointment in our farthest circuit, we must needs have a Choir to spoil our worship, and to drive, by its unearthly screechings, the Spirit of God from our assemblies. So much for the repudiation of our disciplinary law in the case. It has "*improved*" our singing from a hundred voices down to ten. It has "*improved*" it from the lusty, spiritual outgushing melody of a hundred living hearts, "full of glory and of God," down to the dry, mechanical, artistic squeal of a dozen lifeless souls full of pride and the devil.

Also an accompanying evil to lament is the influence this kind of singing has to cast into disuse the more spiritual of our hymns, as least adapted to the taste of those who execute the praises of God for us, and to bring into vogue those less spiritual. This style of singing also threatens to operate injuriously upon our collection of hymns, by demanding in the future, more and more, as it has procured in the past, the exclusion of some of the best of Wesley's Hymns, and the substitution of those of a lighter character. We have nothing like our Hymn Book. The Discipline is not fully explicit on those doctrines most intimately connected with religious experience. Wesley's Sermons are not in the hands of our multitudes. The Hymn Book is the manual of religious doctrine and experience to our people. It is to us, what the Book of Common Prayer is to the Church of England, the sheet anchor of our doctrinal faith and spiritual practice. We have nothing that can supply its place. It is the great bulwark of defence against an indefinite speculative faith on the one hand, and a vagrant fanaticism, misnamed spirituality, on the other. Its province is to melt away the iciness of the one extreme, and to shine away with light that may be felt the *ignis fatuus* of the other. The English Methodists are noted for an intimate acquaintance with Wesley's Hymns. Many can repeat hundreds of them *memoriter*. To this we may largely attribute the correctness of their views on the great distinctive doctrines of Methodism, and the purity of their correspondent spiritual experience. Few among them come short of the true theory of salvation, and fewer still overleap it into the abyss of experimental fanaticism. In contrast with us they have no foolish controversies on the subject of holiness. They have Wesley's hymns in their hearts, and are settled in the doctrines they teach. They have no occasion for controversy in respect to those doctrines. And we too must have the Hymns.— Not only must we prevent their being driven from our possession as a book, but we must prevent their being beguiled from our use as practical songs. We must urge them upon our people—upon all our people—children and all. And in no other way can we give them into their hands than by giving them the liberty to sing in our assemblies. Without this they will not have them. They are largely without them now. *This is our lamentation.*

RECOMMENDATION:—What can be done to restore what is lost? How shall we return to Zion with singing? There are difficulties in the way of no trifling amount. We can endure or overcome hardness as good soldiers, but this impalpable softness, what weapon can penetrate it? Let any attempt be made to correct this evil, by conforming to the Discipline, and instantly all the fathers and mothers, and other relatives of the singers, possibly some of them officers in the Church, are in a rage. Parental pride loves to behold, and to have others behold, its offspring in a conspicuous place engaged in so commendable and religious performances. The lullabies of the children sing the common sense of the parents to sleep, and the voice of the Discipline is silenced by the quavers of a solo. The least show of dissatisfaction with the performances by the preacher is resented with proper indignation. He will instantly, for his temerity, have about his ears "the noise of those who do sing," besides the still more alarming noise of those who do not sing. The size and respectability of the congregation, indeed all the interests of the Church, temporal, spiritual, eternal, are held, or professed to be held, as intimately and mysteriously dependant on the Choir; while all other things are of secondary importance, and one general outcry of ruin and dismay meets the first attempt to assuage this evil. The fathers threaten to starve out the preacher, and the children warblers threaten to find a perch in some other gallery, whose superstitious preachers and antiquated Disciplines will not disturb the musical rookery. These threats usually bring the audacious preacher to terms, and frequently he is constrained thereafter to atone for past indiscretions by supple and extraordinary efforts in behalf of the "improvements" in this musical department of worship. Another obstacle is found in the undisciplinary public connivance at the evil by those in high authority in the Church. We often see accounts in our church papers, of anniversaries, dedications, foundations laid, missionary and other concerts, with exultant notices of separate choral or instrumental music as a part of those most public religious exercises in which bishops, editors, and secretaries take part; while those officers never dream perhaps, that by so doing they impose the barrier of their high example before the inferior clergy in their sincere and humble efforts to keep and not to mend our rules governing the manner of our singing. And in view of their high example, the question meets us, "Why should a preacher in a circuit be more fastidious in the matter than those far superior in worth and dignity?" Such, indeed, are the obstacles in the way of the restitution of the observance of the rules in the case that "whoso is fearful and afraid let him return and depart,"—but to those steadfast in the covenant to observe and enforce the rules of the Church, the Plan and List accompanying this Recommendation is proposed. The Plan has received the sanction of one of the Bishops to whom it was referred in the case of a choral fluctuation in one of our charges. Let the Plan be discreetly explained to the official members, severally, for their approval and co-operation. Then to the chorister. If this be done in the right manner and spirit, and the Choir are not remarkably sensitive, or their relatives sensitive in their behalf, doubtless the thing can be accomplished peacably, without strife or confusion. The only difficulty will be to hold the Choir to the Plan. For before long there will come over them a strong temptation to fall back upon tunes unknown to the congregation, in which they cannot readily join, and then having thus provided the argument, they will labor to discredit the equality or superiority of congregational singing. A sensitive and irreligious Choir will not long endure the contrast which will be the result of a strict adhesion to the Plan. After a little they will be contrasted to death;—at which point it is of the nicest importance that they die an easy and peaceful death, with the careful administration of "extreme unction" of the most oleaginous kind. The only thing is for the preacher to hold them immutably to the Plan; and if necessary to this, let him himself give out the name of the last tune.—All depends upon it, and success invariably results. If the Choir have a religious complexion, and especially if the chorister have a common share of religious and of common sense, they will readily concur in the plan, and harmonious congregational singing, led by competent singers, as contemplated by the Discipline, will be regained. The chief advantages of this Plan are:—It proposes no overt attack on the Choir, to awaken indignation in them or their friends. It is reasonable in demand, asking only one-third of the disciplinary rights of the congregation, without robbing the Choir of any. It is undeniably disciplinary as far as it goes. It is free from any show and fact of strictness and rigidity of administration. Let one-third of the singing be gained, and executed in a good, free, lusty manner, and soon the other two-thirds will be gained also. The congregation will inevitably sing a finical Choir into unison with them or into—nothing. Amen.

PLAN FOR CONGREGATIONAL SINGING.—"The Discipline provides for both choir and congregational singing in connection with each other. It no where recognizes exclusive choir singing. It no where recognizes instrumental music. It admits of no monopoly of singing, any more than it does of speaking in class, or praying in prayer meeting. On the contrary it expressly forbids the use of tunes which, front difficulty of execution are unsuited to the general capacity of the congregation. It even prohibits the introduction of new tunes, except under certain conditions, having respect to the congregation as singers of the same. The exhortation to all the people to sing, and not one in ten only, is solemn mockery by any other construction of the Discipline than the aforesaid.

This inseparable union of both choir and congregational singing is wisely recognized in the Discipline, to guard against the possible excesses of each, respectively, to wit: To guard on the one hand, against the entire abandonment of singing by the congregation, and the substitution therefor, of an artificial style of singing, foreign to our essential economy as a denomination, and in some cases incompatible with the sentiment and spirit of many of our best and most common hymns; and also on the other hand to guard against the irregularity and general vagrancy into which uneducated congregational singing is liable to degenerate. An adherence to the requirements of the Discipline will effectually prevent both of these extremes.

In order therefore to conform more fully to the wise prescriptions of the Discipline, to guard against formality in singing, and to insure its exercise with the spirit and with the understanding also; the Choir, or, as they are termed in the Discipline, the singers, are hereby authorized, exhorted and commanded, to sing the first two hymns of each service in tunes of their own selection, and style, conforming as far as practicable to the provisions of the Discipline, and the congregation are exhorted to join with them as far as they can. This concession is made out of respect to the acknowledged sensitiveness of choirs in general, yet with grave doubts as to its strict accordance with the spirit of the Discipline in the case.

And whereas, the ever varying style of church music, originating in the diversity of text books of the same, the introduction therein of new tunes, and the alteration of old ones, together with the variable manner of its execution by the several music teachers and professors of the science, have heretofore generally operated to prevent the co-operation of the congregation, especially of children and aged people, thus virtually depriving them of their privilege in this part of divine worship: Therefore it is furthermore authorized and demanded that the last hymn of each service, invariably be given out by the preacher, and the doxology when used, be sung in a tune familiar to the congregation, and in a congregational style of singing, without the use of the tune book, without orchestral precision, display, or formality, and in all other possible respects so as to admit of and encourage the most full and easy co-operation of the congregation in the exercise.

And the preacher posesses and may not relinquish without a palpable breach of disciplinary trust, the right to appoint at any time one or more to lead the singing; to indicate tunes appropriate to be sung, and to make such suggestions as in his judgment shall tend to secure most effectually the objects herein above designed."

MISCELLANEOUS OBSERVATIONS.—We need not so much to sing scientifically, as to *sing*. Some choirs are ever learning, and never able to do this. Some choristers even, are unable to start a familiar hymn in class or prayer meeting. The pitch-pipe and the long book are absent; and the chorister's reputation as a musician will not allow him to run the risk of any attempts at singing, without these to him necessary implements. Others are shy of attempting in his august presence, and thus silence reigns. Like every other department of religion, singing is more dependant on practical experience than on scientific theory for excellence. Yet the science is a help to the practice, provided it is managed to be put into practice instead of preventing it. The *American Vocalist* is hereby recommended as the best music text book adapted to the wants of our denomination. Some tunes, excellent to the ear of masters of the science, are impracticable to the common people. They will never learn them. They will never sing them. It is folly to expect it. But there are many tunes, old yet immortal, which the people easily learn, and love to sing. Let such be used; and as fast as a new one is born of the same favorable sort, let it be adopted. Let all ditties be discarded at once and forever. They are almost, not quite, as bad as the scientific canticles of modern choirs. Methodist singing ought to be one mighty chorus; a full song, "fortissimo," of the whole people, and uttered lustily. Some of our hymns are peculiar in metre; they might be termed "Methodist metre." No tunes have yet been found entirely adapted to our hymns, peculiarly Wesleyan, in six lines, eight syllables. We have found as yet but two adapted to general taste, and at the same time to this metre, and the latter only by repeating the last two lines of each verse.— Away with all Boston Singing Books. They seem of set purpose to ignore the spirit and style of Methodist Hymns. Let us ignore them forthwith. By singing the old songs in the old tunes, our people will more readily find, and more joyously walk in the old paths. Let us return to Zion with singing.

SELECTION.

301. O, for a heart to praise my God - - - - - - - - - *Pisgah.*
599. See how great a flame aspires, - - - - - - - - - *Watchman.*
174. There is a fountain filled with blood, - - - - - *Land of Rest.*
559. Come, let us ascend, - - - - - - - - - - - *Happiness.*
95. He dies, the friend of sinners dies, - - - - - - *Bonnie Doon.*
180. Blow ye the trumpet blow, - - - - - - - - - - *Lenox.*
211. Show pity Lord, O Lord forgive, - - - - - - - *Rockingham.*
247. Rock of ages, cleft for me. - - - - - - - - - *Rock of ages.*
252. Father I dare believe, - - - - - - - - - - - *Concord.*
258. And can I yet delay, - - - - - - - - - - - *Boylston.*
264. Now I have found the ground wherein, - - - - - *Duane Street.*
284. Arise my soul, arise, - - - - - - - - - - - *Carmarthen.*
295. O glorious hope of perfect love, - - - - - - - *Hedding.*
300. Love divine, all love excelling, - - - - - - - *Greenville.*

PRACTICAL PROPOSITION No. 5.

"To restore the custom of attendance from abroad upon our Love Feasts."

LAMENTATION :—Alas for our Love-Feasts! How sadly are they neglected! Once they were the chief of our solemn assemblies.—The people came up to them from far and near to present themselves before God. They had a wonderful attraction and drew the people to them. Notwithstanding closed doors and stringent conditions of admission, they were always well attended. Divine manifestations of power and glory were always expected, and almost always realized. But it has ceased to be so now. In most of our charges, now, a Love Feast is little or nothing more, either in numbers or religious interest, than a General Class Meeting—a General Class Meeting breaded and watered—nothing more. In some of our cities and villages, as if unfit, in their emaciated state, to be seen by daylight, our Love Feasts are crowded away into basement rooms, on Saturday nights. This on the plea that they will be more quiet and not interfere with, or be interfered with by the regular and more respectable services of the Sabbath. This object is doubtless secured. Quiet enough they are. Some of our preachers, out of respect to the example of other enlightened denominations, and to the improved civilization of Methodism, are desirous to abandon them altogether as a religious anomaly of the age. The ticket system is already obsolete. Preachers and Leaders are too much occupied with other duties to distribute the tickets regularly. Open doors have made empty houses. An inevitable consequence also of open doors, except the Love Feast be hid in some basement room, is that it is always annoyed by the ingress of persons coming to the more public performances. The solemn banqueting room is made the vestibule thoroughfare to the rear boxes and the galleries of the sacred theatre. Presiding Elders cast all the responsibility of this on the Preachers; while in return the Preachers disclaim all the responsibility, and insist that the Love Feast is the Presiding Elder's meeting. So between them both there is no order about the thing. Some Preachers have attempted to conduct them in conformity with the Discipline; and thereby have raised a tempest against themselves in the charge, and complaints of harshness and rigidity in the conference. Dilatory members, or dignified owners of pews, arriving too late, after rattling and banging the doors awhile, go away mortally insulted and abused by this observance of the Discipline. The Presiding Elder, always a safe and conservative man, thinks the Preacher lacking in discretion and prudence; not of course because the door was closed according to the Discipline, but because somebody got offended by being shut out; and so represents the case in the Bishop's Council; and as the reward of his conscientious effort to fulfill his solemn ordination vows in the case, the Preacher, as a troubler in Israel, is sent to some backwoods circuit, where there are no meeting houses, and consequently no Love Feast doors to give him, or anybody else any trouble. So that in these days, in this Conference, no Preacher dare restore the ticket system, or attempt closed doors, for fear of rebellion in his charge, scandal in the Conference, and representations of injudiciousness in the Cabinet.

"If the foundations be removed, what can the righteous do?" When those among us occupying chief offices, and others occupying chief charges, totally ignore the Discipline in respect to Love Feasts, what can be done by inferior preachers? The despairing answer from each is, "If others would observe the Discipline, I would too; but what is the use of trying it alone?" This is the ready apology for every breach of disciplinary duty. Many of us would be glad to fulfil our ordination vows to observe the Rules of the Church, but dare not attempt it *alone*. Hence the reason for this (so called) Nazarite Union. Our bread is in our mouth, and our reputation and appointments are swayed by the breath of good men, to be sure, but of men exceedingly sensitive to the unsafeness of such as offend any in their charge by the enforcement of the Discipline. This is known to us, and the legitimate result of such knowledge is to induce in us a tacit determination not to weary and expose ourselves in a hopeless strife to recover the lost supremacy of the Discipline over our Love Feasts. There it rests at present. There, for the present, we propose to let it rest. We might get along with the people in the matter, for most of them are with us on this point,— but there is no resisting superior ministerial influence and example. "Shall the potsherd strive with him who made it?" All that we can recommend at present is merely remedial. A radical restitution is impracticable under the adverse circumstances above indicated. *This is our lamentation.*

RECOMMENDATION:—Our charges are generally small in extent and convenient for intercommunication. Nevertheless we have become segregated, not only literally by dislocation, but in our spiritual sympathies. The social religious sentiment always expires with the decease of our practical itineracy. Both are virtually extinct in most charges in this Conference. And we fear the most we can do in respect to this Practical Proposition, may be but a kind of temporary tonic, hopelessly, yet kindly administered, to awaken into something like life, the social religious principle from that lethargy which is the fatal token of approaching death. Yet by united and persistent effort a sensible alleviation may be accomplished, which, in the end, by the favor of God, may grow up into a ground of hope for the restitution of our Love Feasts to something like their early condition. This object, hopeless as it may now seem, is worth the experiment of all the means within our power. Let us make our Love Feasts as valuable as we can; and such increased value, appreciated as it will be, may encourage preachers and people to replace around them those ancient guards, which at present they are hardly worth possessing.

Therefore, with exceeding shame at the smallness of the recommendation, it is recommended that we violently extol the institution before the people; that we publicly notify in our congregations the quarterly meetings on adjoining charges convenient, and exhort our people to attend the same: and that we invite publicly and privately the membership of contiguous charges to attend ours; providing for their entertainment after the manner of former years. Let the Saturday evening Quarterly Meeting prayer meeting be invariably maintained against the intrusion of all other religious services.—Even if a Bishop be present, let him pray, but not preach. Among other incidental advantages resulting from the prevalence of this recommendation, that of increased quarterly collections will be one. Meanwhile we commend to your consideration, as a further and future measure, the propriety and practicability of closed doors; and ultimately the ticket system. *This is our recommendation.*

PRACTICAL PROPOSITION No. 6.

"To restore more fully the custom of Camp Meetings among us."

LAMENTATION:—Alas for the incubus which rests upon us! A dry formality has come gradually over us, pervading our entire worship. Our assemblies in many of our sanctuaries feel the constraints of the place and can enjoy religion any where else better than in the house of God. A cold and respectable solemnity, like the atmosphere of an Egyptian night, dry, but felt, chills the fervor of devotion. Religious feelings must be restrained within the bounds of modern decency and order. Spiritual emotion may exhibit itself, if it must, in the class room, and in the prayer meeting, where the elite of the church and congregation never enter; but it must not manifest itself in the chief room of the temple. There it must be still and known that Satan is God. There to kneel is vulgar,—to say "Amen!" is sacrilege,—and to shout is the *ne plus ultra* of fanatical madness. We have become shorn of our strength, and like unto the nations around about us.

Other denominations can worship quite agreeably under bonds, for they were born with bands upon them. But not so we. We were free born. Ours is a free salvation or none. And our worship must be free or none. The bands of this formality are upon the neck of the daughter of our people. All she can do is to sit in stony silence and feel nothing—but the constraint that is upon her. The thunder of the captains, and the shoutings, "the noise in the house of the Lord, as in the day of a solemn feast," is hushed as in a charnel. There they sit side by side, the skeleton dead of the daughter of our people, embalmed, not, to be sure, in frankincense and myrrh, and ancient dust, but bandaged instead in costly broadcloth, and silk and satin, and emitting as the odor of their lifeless sanctity, the fragrance of lavendar and pomatum. Many of our sanctuaries have come to be but sacred theatres for the regular and decent performance of the drama of christian worship. The preacher reads or recites his allotted part, the orchestra furnishes the interlude performances, the sexton collects the coppers to foot the bill of incidental expenses, and the solemn play is ended with the apostolic benediction. All, however sincere and well intended, is merely intellectual, respectable, artistic,—without a soul, and without a sign of spiritual life and power. Let an effort be made by the preacher for a revival, and it meets this fatal obstacle,—this spiritual nothingness. Some may become serious in the prayer meetings, or at their homes, but let them enter the audience room of the sanctuary and all feeling is gone in a moment. God is not there,—he never frequents the theatre. And where He is not salvation is not,—for salvation is of the Lord. Not that in most places, as yet, or in all points above recited, is this the lamentable condition of our worship, but more or less this condition of things is prevalent and increasing among us. It is already frequent, and threatens to become general. *This is our lamentation.*

RECOMMENDATION:—Since, as lamented, the people cannot find God in his sanctuaries, at least some of them, where shall they go to find him? Since the half-living membership—living dead men —languish and perish in the God forsaken gates of Zion, where shall they go to breathe a freer atmosphere, haply to bring their fainting souls back from the shades of spiritual death? "The groves were God's first temples," and he has never forsaken them. In them, when not elsewhere, there is "freedom to worship God." It is a strange contrast of opposite causes producing the same result that the want of houses of worship in early days, and the possession of houses of worship in modern days, controlled and conditioned as they are, drove us to the use of Camp Meetings then, and compels us to the same resort now. It is nevertheless true. The Jews had their annual Feast of Tabernacles, even after the temple was built. The new structure did not abrogate the ancient custom. The pious from all parts of the land gathered to this feast. The social religious sentiment of the people was kept alive, and nourished by it, until Jereboam made Israel to sin by segregating the people apart in their worship.

Brethren, there must be general gatherings of our people together. It must be, or we perish from before the Lord. By the work being cut up into small circuits and stations, the connexional principle in our economy is violated and almost destroyed. The watchmen can hardly see eye to eye, and our people can hardly see one another at all. This has been laying the axe to the root of the tree of Methodism. The virtual abrogation of the itineracy is the virtual abrogation of Methodism. Its substantial unity is hewn down in this Conference, and as a denomination we shall yet learn that it is easier and quicker work to fell a goodly tree than to replace it again, by nursing into growth a shoot from its roots. We repeat, the connexional principle is nearly extinct among us. Our Love Feasts are not, as formerly, general gatherings of our people. They are little more than voluntary general class meetings for the society where they are held. They do not serve as occasions to draw the people together in numbers adequate to maintain and perpetuate the manifested fellowship of saints. The Camp Meeting is our only resort to supply this want. And the result has justified the experiment. The spiritual condition of those charges among us most largely in attendance on those lately held, is an unanswerable vindication of their utility for good. To charges where for years a lamentable deadness had prevailed, those attending the Camp Meeting, accompanied by those there converted, have returned carrying with them the sacred flame to spread like fire in a dry stubble. This is the general happy result. In some cases, however, where merely formal godliness had entrenched itself with extraordinary strength it has been able, aided by ministerial and official support, to resist the gracious invasion, and extinguish the kindling fires of spiritual devotion with showers of obloquy, descending in epithets of "wildfire," "delusion," "fanaticism," and such like opprobrious names, appropriate from such sources to all manifestations of religious zeal and power.

There is another consideration of special import:—every Camp Meeting conducted in the true "old line Methodist" manner and spirit is a mighty stride of the people back toward the old paths.— It affords such a signal contrast between freedom and simplicity of worship on the one hand, and the constraint and deadness of artificial worship on the other, as is no where else to be seen;—a demonstration as vital to the former as fatal to the latter. It is therefore recommended to extol Camp Meetings everywhere, especially before those preachers opposed to them; to resist boldly to the face all who oppose and ridicule them; and to do this with exceeding zeal and audacity; to exhort and encourage our people to attend them; to labor discreetly in our district associations that they may be held under the most favorable auspices as to time, place and circumstances; to attend ourselves, not merely to preach a sermon, but to be active and abundant in our respective society tents, in all the exercises of the occasion; and to avail ourselves instantly and decisivly in the cause of God, of any good influence that may return with our people from them. *This is our recommendation.*

CAUTION:—Inasmuch as in these days of pseudo religious respectability, the charge of extravagance and fanaticism, as it ever has been in certain quarters, will continue to be urged against those who have religion enough to feel it and speak of it earnestly; it behooves us to give no just occasion for the charge aforesaid. Let us be aware and assured, that the least extravagance, however innocent, will be greedily caught at and outcried through all the length and breadth of the land, for the sake of casting a stigma upon Camp Meetings in general, but more particularly upon us, brethren, who are known to be their chief advocates and supporters in the Conference. Let us not be surprised, or unsettled in our purpose, if these charges come, not from infidels and scoffers, as might be expected, but from members of our own church and ministry. And when we hear it from this source, let us restrain all indignation, remembering that prejudices derived from circumstances and foreign associations, rather than any willful and malicious pravity, ought to be their apology in the case. Let us therefore guard ourselves and the people against any extravagance of manner, or censoriousness of speech; that no real offence may be given. Let us keep them in their expressions of experience, as far as possible, to that form of sound words maintained by the Bible, the Discipline, the Hymn Book, and Wesley's Sermons. This to avoid misapprehension and whatever of religious scandal may be consequent therefrom. Yet all this in such a way as in no wise to restrain the proper and true exercise of that spiritual freedom which is the heritage of those "whom the Son makes free." For ourselves, brethren, as is our right, and our bounden duty, let us not so dread any imputation of fanaticism, or any other opprobrious charge, as to shun declaring the whole counsel of God, and testifying with exceeding boldness against whatever exalteth it-self against the Cross of Christ. *This is our caution.*

PRACTICAL PROPOSITION No. 7.

"To Restore the custom in part of free seats in our houses of worship."

LAMENTATION:—Alas, " Our houses are turned to aliens!" Judas sold the Son of God; we do a little better; we sell only the house of God. The sale of pews, growing prevalent among us, formerly against the Discipline, and always against the general custom of the Church, is the most fatal of all our evils, and the most imprac-ticable to eradicate. It cannot be rectified in a day. Freedom is the natural birthright of the sanctuary in which a free Salvation is proclaimed; and when sold "for a mess of pottage," it is gone for-ever. Repentance is in vain. We have bound ourselves with legal obligations which we cannot shake off at pleasure; even after we have become convinced of the ruinous mistake we have made.—While other denominations are retracing their course, and freeing their houses as fast as possible, we are greedily enslaving ours; heedless of the caution furnished by the past experience of others.

Among us as a denomination, the selling of pews has been evil and only evil continually. It is an evil root that branches out its bitterness in every direction. It has made empty houses; in gen-eral those purchasing pews are those most rarely in the house of God. Frequently owners of pews remove from the charge; or un-able to hear the truth faithfully administered, (provided such faith-fulness were allowable in such houses) they leave in anger; and for a long time their pews remain an unsightly vacancy in the house of God; or they sell them at a discount to such as rarely attend wor-ship. This emptiness is almost always observable by contrast in a house where part of the pews are sold, and part free. The free part is always full, while in the other part, here and there a solemn nabob sits and sleeps.

The selling of pews also interferes with the free exercise of some parts of our worship. We always, virtually, accompany our deed of sale of pews with the addition of a bond and mortgage upon our freedom to worship God. The fact of sold pews is more or less incompatible with the free exercise of our worship, as prescribed by the Discipline, and commended by the usages of our Church.—This " saving clause" in the deed of sale is a mere form: Our wor-ship is enslaved nevertheless. A prayer meeting is in a constrained and awkward position in such a house. The members are scattered here and there. The most spiritual and efficient are frequently crowded far into the rear, or driven into corners; while the whole membership is interspersed with the proud and ungodly proprietors of pews, too unmannerly to kneel, too self-sufficient to pray; the cash constituted overseers of the flock, who literally watch over it in all its exercises of devotion. Who ever knew a lively and spiritual prayer meeting in such a house, and under such circumstances. The thing is impossible in the fitness of things.

Pew selling also interferes with singing. Those who should in some manner sit together and lead the singing, are scattered apart, and find therein an apology for getting up into the gallery, usually above the atmosphere of grace, to "perform" the singing there.

Pew selling is also a breach of the gospel equality of believers.— It robs a poor saint of his equal rights, to accommodate the pride of a rich sinner. It places money before grace. It crowds the poor into inferior places, or out of the house altogether. It virtually prohibits our preaching the gospel to the poor. They will not come to our assemblies as notorious paupers, crawling into some corner to hear, or to be graciously taken in by some pompous pew owner, as an ostentatious act of condescension. The poor not members of our church, never come to such houses. They have no right there. It is private property. God has no right there; we have sold him out of house and home; and have driven his poor, whom he gave to have always with us, into the streets on the sabbath; into the dens of intemperance and infamy, or to glean haply a little gospel truth, uttered by street preachers, under the defense of police, bludgeons and revolvers.

Pew selling also ignores our ancient and decent custom, once disciplinary, of the sitting of men and women apart in our congregations. We can without any trouble enforce this custom in school houses, court houses, barns, private dwellings, at camp-meetings— anywhere but in houses of worship ostensibly owned by the Methodist Episcopal Church. This decent custom, everywhere approved spontaneously by the common sense of all decent people, is prevalent in all congregations of people civilized and savage, except in circuses, theatres and churches.

We hold that no arguments, however specious, are valid against the above array of evils. All such arguments originate in pride and sham aristocracy, or in a mean and craven desire to please the rich and purchase the honor of their attendance on our worship, at the expense of the equal rights of others. The selling of pews is a great evil, and has slowly and surely rooted out Methodism wherever it has prevailed; it is one of the chief causes of the decrease of membership, and the decay of piety in many of the principal stations among us. *This is our Lamentation.*

RECOMMENDATION:—Such is the present mania for stock Churches, and for the selling and renting of pews among us, that it is advisable in all cases to oppose a legal barrier to it as soon as possible; but in attempting this, great caution must be used, and no false motions made. It will not do to trust to any past indefinite understanding or agreements not to sell; these have been found of little amount as obstacles to sale or rent, when the preacher, seconded by aristocratic members and outside influence, sets himself to violate the discipline and custom of the church in the case. It will not do to trust the verbal promises of Trustees not to sell, such promises may not be held as binding by their successors in office. Corporations are forgetful, and the only sure faith to be kept with them is that which is signed, sealed, delivered, acknowledged and recorded.

Some preachers have a wonderful faculty of getting houses built or repaired, or some finical fixtures added, and then, to liquidate the expense, propose and urge the sale of the pews, and all who follow on the charge, find the fatal embarrassments herein above lamented. An irreverable curse is laid upon the house forever; it is mortgaged, to the world, the flesh and the devil, beyond the power of redemption. "Christ, Belial & Co." would be altogether too religious in signification, to be an appropriate inscription over its portals; every house thus sold is a mausoleum "to Methodist Discipline, if not to Methodist Doctrine also."

The people are sometimes frivolous, and easily brought to favor the innovation of selling pews; the pride of some prompts in the same direction; the parsimoniousness of some prompts them to sell rather than contribute for a free house. In some of our charges Trustees are men of lax Methodistic principles, and care nothing for church discipline or custom, when they happen to contravene their notions; but after all, the ministry are the most responsible for the prevalence of this evil, it is an exotic upas of their engrafting upon the tree of Methodism.

Never lift a finger to build, purchase or repair a house, unless an equal part of it be free, and such freedom adequately secured by legal obligations on record. Never give a dollar to redeem one from under the sheriff's hammer, except on the above condition.— Let it be sold, it is not God's house. Suffer no contributions to be taken in your charge, unless every subscription be conditioned on this point. Let no moving appeals move from this fixed position; it is a cruel mercy that would be pitiful here—with as much reason you might pity "a house of merchandise," or "a den of thieves."

It is worse to sell than to rent, for in the latter case there is some chance, though small probability of reclaiming the freedom of the house, when we shall have reclaimed our senses. As a choice of evils the renting may produce an annual revenue for repairs or other purposes. When applied to the preacher's salary, it has never in the long run, proved as sure and profitable as the usual way of raising the same by apportionment or subscription. Let no preacher's opinion be deceived and bought by this specious bribe. Liberal contributions for the support of the Gospel, and for benevolent purposes, are never fostered by this kind of traffic in sanctuary rights and privileges.

Let this evil be ended; at least, let it spread no further; we can stop it—as one man let us do it, or it will stop Methodism. Accompanying this document is a deed of the freedom of the side seats of any house of worship. The deed has been examined and pronounced valid by competent lawyers. It secures to all named in it severally, the indiscriminate right to occupy any of the seats deeded. This precludes all subsequent trustees from renting or selling the same exclusively to others. Let each of us discreetly sound the several trustees of the houses in our respective charges, as to their willingness to acknowledge the deed. If a majority refuse, let the thing pass quietly by, and in the meantime let us discreetly use our influence to have those elected who will agree to the measure.— Let us all begin instantly, and persevere till the thing is accomplished everywhere; let there be a concert in this, if it cannot be done this year, it may be done hereafter; let it be done as soon as possible; in three years every house in the conference, now free, ought to be secured inviolate forever. Such is the furor among some in the ministry to enslave our houses of worship, that their freedom is in jeopardy every hour. It will soon be too late; extraordinary caution and precision will be necessary; let us make no false motions; let us make no delay.

A true copy of the Deed can always be had of our Recorder. It is of prime importance that the names of the three members of conference be inserted; this, so that in case all the others should be persuaded to relinquish their right and title under the Deed, these will hold on, and retain the freedom. Scribes will give all necessary instruction as to the manner of the thing. Let all Deeds, acknowledged and recorded, be transmitted to our Recorder, for custody and future reference. Ultimately at the pleasure of the conference, they can be placed in the conference trunk; as in some sense conference documents.

CAUTION:—It is obvious that extraordinary *discretion* is advisable in respect to this document, both because of the paramount importance of the thing, and also in respect to the anticipated obstacles, which interested persons, if cognizant of the purpose, might interpose against the accomplishment of the object proposed. Acts. xxiii : 22.

DEED.

THIS INDENTURE, made this first day of June, in the year of our Lord one thousand eight hundred and fifty-five, between A B, C D, E F, G H, I J, K L, and M N, of the town of A, in the County of B, in the State of New York, Trustees of the First Methodist Episcopal Society, of the town of A., in the County of B., in the State of New York, of the first part: and. A. B, C D, E. F, G. H, I. J, K. L, M N, O P, Q R, S T, U V, W X, and Y Z, of the same place, members of the Methodist Episcopal Society aforesaid; and B. C, D, E, and F. G, members of the Genesee Conference of the Methodist Episcopal Church of the second part:

WITNESSETH: That the said party of the first part in consideration of the sum of one dollar, to them in hand paid, the receipt wh reof is hereby acknowledged; and in further consideration of the peace and quiet of said society, by securing equal accommodation to all the members thereof in the house of God during divine service therein, and in obedience to the customs and discipline of the Methodist Episcopal Church in the case:—

Have granted, and by these presents do grant and convey to the said party of the second part, their heirs, and assigns forever, and to each and several of them, the full equal, right, privilege and freedom to occupy indiscriminately, as attendants on divine worship in a decent and orderly manner, in accordance with the discipline and usages of the Methodist Episcopal Church, any and several of all the side slips, seats, or pews of the meeting house of the Methodist Episcopal Society aforesaid; and to the said party of the second part the free use and exercise of the said right, freedom and privilege the said party of the first part will forever Warrant and Defend.

(L. S.)
(L. S.)
(L. S.)
(L. S.)
(L. S.)

www.ingramcontent.com/pod-product-compliance
Lightning Source LLC
Chambersburg PA
CBHW030307030426
42337CB00012B/619